Afghanistan's
Heroic Artists

Rob Waring, *Series Editor*

HEINLE
CENGAGE Learning™

Australia • Brazil • Japan • Korea • Mexico • Singapore • Spain • United Kingdom • United States

Words to Know

This story is set in the country of Afghanistan and takes place in its capital city, Kabul. It also refers to conditions in Bamiyan [bɑmiɑn], a region outside of Kabul.

A **National Treasures.** Read the sentences. Then complete the paragraph with the correct forms of the underlined words.

An archive is a collection of records, books, or films of historical interest.
A carving is a piece of art shaped by cutting it with artistry and exactness.
A country's heritage is its history, traditions, and culture.
A landmark is a historical building or other point of interest.
An oil painting is a painting produced with oil-based paints.

From 1996 to 2001, a religious group called the Taliban ruled Afghanistan. During this period, this strict regime destroyed several historically important (1) _____, including buildings and statues. In the Bamiyan region, they tore down huge ancient statues. These detailed (2) _____ dated from A.D. 507, and were listed as Afghan national treasures. Later, the Taliban began to destroy the famous and historic (3) _____ hanging in the nation's art galleries and the films stored in the (4) _____ of a central film organization. This tragedy continued until a group of artists decided to act in order to save their country's national (5) _____ .

Oil Paintings at the National Gallery, Kabul.

B **Unusual Heroes.** Read the paragraph. Then complete the definitions with the correct words in **bold**.

During the Taliban years, many artistic works were at risk for being destroyed by the religious police because of their subject matter. Afghan artist Mohammad Yousef Asefi [mouhʌməd yusɛf asɛfi] managed to plan and implement a brilliant **plot** to protect the oil paintings at the National Gallery in Kabul. He succeeded in the **deception** by painting over the oil images with **watercolors** thereby disguising them. Meanwhile, at the National Film Archive, three filmmakers, Kirimi, [kɪrimi], Mustafa [mʊstɑfɑ], and Sadaqui [sɑdɑki], used their **ingenuity** to hide several films that were of national and historic importance. These men could have been killed for their acts, but luckily they lived to become highly **acclaimed** heroes of the art world.

1. A _____ is a secret plan to do something that is forbidden.

2. _____ is one's ability to skillfully solve problems.

3. _____ means to be much admired.

4. _____ causes someone to believe something that is not true.

5. _____ are colors used for painting pictures that are mixed with water, instead of oil, and which can be easily washed away.

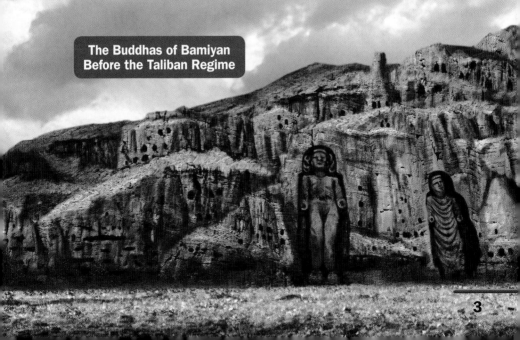

The Buddhas of Bamiyan
Before the Taliban Regime

Between the years of 1996 and 2001, a **fundamentalist**[1] religious group called the Taliban ruled the country of Afghanistan. The group became known for their violence and their strict devotion to rigid interpretations of the rules of the Islamic religion. During their period of control, they slowly began to destroy ancient, historic, and religious landmarks and pieces of art throughout the country. These seemingly senseless acts were committed by the group in an attempt to rid the country of items that were not accepted as part of their strict religious interpretations.

In early 2001, in an act that shocked the rest of the world, the extremist group destroyed the **Buddhas**[2] of Bamiyan, which were located about 225 kilometers* from Afghanistan's capital city, Kabul. The Buddhas were giant statues—the largest existing examples of standing Buddha carvings in the world—built between A.D. 507 and 554. They were perhaps the most famous cultural landmarks of the region, and their location had been listed as a **World Heritage Site**.[3] It was after this terrible destruction of one of the country's most important cultural landmarks that doctor and famous Afghan artist Mohammad Yousef Asefi realized that the entire nation's artistic works were under attack.

---

[1] **fundamentalist:** someone who follows the rules of a religion or organization very strictly and exactly
[2] **Buddha:** the symbol of Buddhism, a religion of east and central Asia
[3] **World Heritage Site:** an important cultural place, chosen for preservation by the United Nations Educational, Scientific, and Cultural Organization (UNESCO)
*See page 32 for a metric conversion chart.

CD 2, Track 01

The Buddhas of Bamiyan were destroyed by the Taliban in early 2001.

6

As Taliban rule continued, Dr. Asefi began to wonder—and worry—what would be destroyed next. He talks about his feelings at that time. "I became very sad," he says, "when I heard that the statue[s] in Bamiyan had been destroyed. A rumor was spreading that the artwork exhibited in the National Gallery and the National Museum would be the next victim." The Taliban condemned statues or paintings that represented living things, such as people, and their plan at the time was to destroy all artistic works featuring such subject matter.

Asefi is a medical doctor and a well-known Afghan painter for whom all artistic works—especially oil paintings—hold a special meaning. As one watches him paint, carefully placing various shades of color in exact places as he creates one of his works, it becomes clear that for Asefi, creating a work of art requires not only creativity, but time and patience. That's why the Taliban's rule of terror really **hit home**[4] for him when the artwork at the presidential palace and the ministry of foreign affairs was **slashed**[5] and destroyed by the Taliban regime. Asefi became extremely distressed when he learned that some of the paintings that had been permanently damaged were his own.

---

[4]**hit home:** become personal or real
[5]**slash:** make a long deep cut with something sharp

Asefi explains how miserable he felt when he discovered that his paintings had been attacked. "I had painted my paintings with a lot of delicacy," he says, "and now they were torn up or destroyed beyond repair." After making this comment, he mentions the one question that kept coming to his mind after hearing of the tragic event: "How could this happen?" It was a question for which there was no simple answer.

With not only his own paintings, but all of the paintings at the National Gallery now at risk from the Taliban's religious police, Asefi formulated a plan that could easily have resulted in his death. The Taliban was a **brutal**[6] regime, and one that had no hesitation about dealing quickly and violently with anyone or anything that did not follow its strict, structured interpretations of Islamic religious law.

In order to implement his plan, Asefi first volunteered for a job in the National Gallery. He was hired to restore paintings that had been damaged during the wars that had **plagued**[7] the country during the years preceding the Taliban's rule. Once inside the gallery, Asefi needed an **accomplice**,[8] somebody who would help him to carry out his clever plan. He found one in a man named Enayet, a member of the National Gallery staff who shared Asefi's **contempt**[9] for the Taliban and his courage to take them on. Risking their lives, Enayet and other staff members brought endangered paintings to the room where Asefi worked. It was there that the real ingenuity of the plan became apparent.

---

[6]**brutal:** extremely violent and without care regarding others
[7]**plague:** upset with repeated disturbances or interruptions
[8]**accomplice:** a partner in committing an illegal or unacceptable act
[9]**contempt:** dislike; hatred

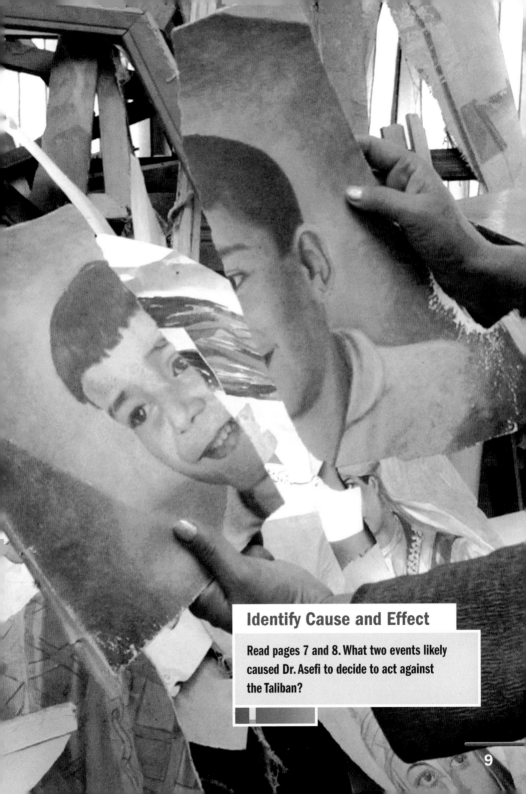

Identify Cause and Effect

Read pages 7 and 8. What two events likely caused Dr. Asefi to decide to act against the Taliban?

The plot that Dr. Asefi and his accomplices formulated was quite simple. Since the Taliban forbade paintings that illustrated living things, Dr. Asefi simply made the offensive elements of the paintings—the living things—disappear. He explains his daring plan. "I suddenly came up with the thought of using watercolors on top of oil paintings to hide the unacceptable parts," he says. Month after month, Asefi and his accomplices ran an 'art-rescue' factory right under the noses of Taliban religious police.

Enayet explains how they fooled the Taliban during the religious police's unexpected visits to the gallery. "Whenever they would come," he says, "I would lock the door. The doctor was inside. He would stop his work, having understood that somebody was here. Naturally I was afraid because the Taliban were everywhere." If the Taliban had found out what they were doing, both men—and other members of the staff—almost certainly would have been punished by death.

watercolors

Ultimately, Asefi's art-rescue team placed about 80 paintings back on display in the Gallery, all of them repainted so that any 'improper' parts were covered by watercolors. Amazingly, the Taliban inspectors never noticed the team's deception. Then, when the Taliban's brutal regime came to an end in 2001, museum staff members simply wiped off the watercolors from the oil paintings, and the rescued treasures were once again in full view, in some cases for the first time in generations.

As he stands in a room surrounded by beautiful works of classic Afghani art, Asefi talks about what he and his friends managed to accomplish. "Despite all the suffering and hard work," he reports, "our goal was to change something and we did it." But Dr. Asefi's clever deception wasn't the only plot that succeeded during the days of the Taliban …

Later, museum staff members simply wiped off the watercolors to reveal the hidden paintings.

At the national film archive in Kabul, which is called 'Afghan Films,' a group of filmmakers watches a show of film treasures that were once thought to be completely lost. As they view the precious scenes that were saved from the hands of destruction, one can see the emotion and pride in the faces of these unusual 'film heroes.' The fact that they can still watch these films—and show them to others—is evidence of their own brilliant creativity, ingenuity, and bravery.

During the time of the Taliban, these artists were also victimized by the group's extreme religious interpretations and the constant threat of having thousands of original film works destroyed because of their content. Fortunately, like Dr. Asefi and the staff at the National Gallery, these filmmakers were able to pull off a clever deception that ensured that the entire film archive would not be destroyed. Their incredible story started on the terrible day when the religious police came to burn all the films in the archive.

The filmmakers became very anxious when they realized that the films—national treasures in the art form that they loved—might be completely destroyed. "We were very upset when the minister of the Taliban brought the order to burn the films," says Kirimi, one of the filmmakers. "We felt our hearts **pounding**.[10] We became emotional."

When the police arrived, the filmmakers were forced to turn over hundreds of pieces of film, which were then burned to piles of ashes by the religious police. Another filmmaker named Mustafa shows the **ditch**[11] where the religious police burned the films right in front of him and the other artists. "Here," he says, gesturing to a dry hollow in the earth. "They burned the films here," he says. "We have the evidence. They burned them in front of me. That day, it was like a dearest friend [was] being killed in front of [us]. That day was the darkest and hardest day for us."

While the loss of the films was an emotional event for all of the artists, for some it was even more than that. Kirimi and Mustafa's colleague Sadaqui adds that for him, the situation almost became violent due to the strength of feelings triggered by the actions of the religious police. "I became irrational," he explains. "I decided to throw myself and the Minister of Information and Culture into the fire with the films." Luckily, his colleagues prevented the disaster. "At that moment, one of my colleagues **grabbed**[12] me and stopped me," he says.

---

[10] **pound:** beat strongly
[11] **ditch:** a long narrow hole dug in the earth, especially to hold or carry water
[12] **grab:** take quickly and roughly

While the artists were obviously upset by the Taliban's actions, they had a secret about which the Taliban had no idea. The staff had only given the religious police film prints, which are just copies of the original film and can be replaced, not **film negatives**,[13] which cannot be replaced. Unfortunately, after this first search the Taliban's intense desire to rid the world of what they perceived as unacceptable film images remained. The group made several more trips to the national film archive in order to find and destroy these supposed negative influences. As they did so, the filmmakers became increasingly worried about the safety of the films in their care. When there were no prints left to burn, they knew the religious police would come and throw the negative archive into the fire, too. It was only a matter of time.

The period was terrifying for all those involved with protecting the country's film history, and it was a time that called for courageous action. It was at this point when the small group of film archivists became real heroes. "We all had the same idea," explains Sadaqui, "that we had to preserve the archive of Afghan film at any price, even by paying with our lives." But how were they going to hide the main archive, some 2,900 rolls of irreplaceable negatives, from the eyes of the religious police? It was a huge amount of film to **conceal**,[14] and a mission for which they would be killed if caught.

---

[13]**film negative:** the material in a film camera upon which images are recorded and from which all copies of the material are made
[14]**conceal:** hide or keep something secret, especially through tricks

Predict

Answer the questions using information you have read up to this point. Then check your answers on pages 21 through 24.

1. How did the men hide the film negatives?

2. How successful were they in protecting the nation's film archives?

The filmmakers' plan was simple—brilliantly simple. Mustafa reveals how they did it as he walks quickly down a dark corridor in the Afghan Films building. When he finally arrives at a small door at the very end of the hallway, he pauses to explain. Behind the door lies the country's entire national film archive negatives. Its most extensive film history locked behind one thin barrier. It is here that Mustafa reveals the brilliance of their plot: they hid the archive by hiding the entire room. He describes the plan. "In order for no one to notice the door, we installed wallboard from here," he says gesturing to the floor, "to the ceiling ... here," indicating the top of the corridor. The area behind the wallboard was virtually concealed from view—including the door of the archive room.

With the entrance to the room safely hidden behind board, the next step for the group was to finalize the appearance of the area so that the room would not be visible to the interfering eyes of the religious police. Sadaqui talks about how they ensured that the room wasn't discovered. "With the help of an electrician," he explains, "we also **disabled**[15] the lighting system so that the wall was darkened." While it sounds extremely basic, the plan worked. The religious police walked past the false wall dozens of times and never suspected that there was a room just beyond it.

---

[15]**disable:** make unable to perform; stop something from working

The film rescuers' lives were safe as long as their deception held. But if the Taliban ever found the hidden film negatives, there was no doubt that the men would be put to death. Mustafa remembers how frightening those times were: "The Taliban told us that, even if a small piece of film was found, we will hang you or shoot you in the ditch where the archive was burned." Kirimi confirms his colleague's report, "The Taliban minister said, 'If we find another film here, we will burn it along with you.'" The threats of death did little to discourage the group of brave heroes although there may have been moments when they wanted to give up, especially when the Taliban police were so persistent. The artists remained brave and risked being discovered by one of the world's most feared regimes.

The Taliban surrounds one of its victims.

For many months, the film rescuers endured what seemed like a nightmare. The Taliban's demand for films to burn seemed to have no end, and they conducted several surprise inspections of the building in search of hidden or banned films. Month after month, the staff of Afghan Films suffered through the inspections, terrified that their secret would be discovered. They wondered when it was all going to end.

Finally, the Taliban regime collapsed and their reign of terror and destruction was over. It was a time of extreme joy, but also one of sadness for many film lovers as members of the Afghan general public assumed that the entire film archive had been destroyed by religious police. This sense of sadness soon turned to great enthusiasm when, to everyone's surprise, the archive's rescuers brought the negatives out of hiding. The enormous film archive had been saved and Afghanistan's film heritage was safe.

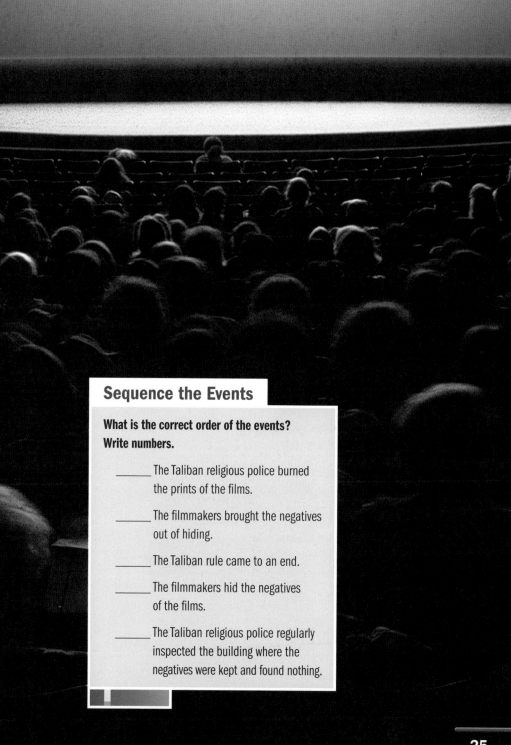

Sequence the Events

What is the correct order of the events?
Write numbers.

_____ The Taliban religious police burned the prints of the films.

_____ The filmmakers brought the negatives out of hiding.

_____ The Taliban rule came to an end.

_____ The filmmakers hid the negatives of the films.

_____ The Taliban religious police regularly inspected the building where the negatives were kept and found nothing.

The filmmakers at Afghan Films were hailed as being heroes, acclaimed for their brave efforts to save the history of Afghan filmmaking for future generations. However, all the excitement meant nothing to them. The courageous men were modest about what they had managed to achieve with their ingenuity. They had done it purely for their love of film and their desire to save the years of work from previous filmmakers. They did, however, save their black-and-white Taliban identification cards as a reminder of a time when they would have given their lives for the art they love.

As they display the small black-and-white identification cards—reminders of another, sadder time—the men smile broadly, proud of their accomplishment and proud of the fact that the film archive still exists. Sadaqui sums up their attitude towards what they did: "Even if we lost our heads, it would have been an honor and privilege. But we didn't allow our heritage to be destroyed. Why? A country that has no culture has no history."

After You Read

1. The destruction of the Buddhas of Bamiyan is an example of what?
   A. an unfortunate accident in Afghanistan
   B. the Taliban's contempt for certain works of art
   C. an artist's failure to save an important landmark
   D. the unification of religion and culture

2. Dr. Asefi formulated a plan to prevent the _____ destruction of oil paintings at the National Gallery.
   A. ongoing
   B. so-called
   C. forthcoming
   D. underlying

3. Which of the following is an appropriate heading for the last paragraph on page 8?
   A. Unemployed Painter Takes Gallery Job
   B. Doctor Plots to Fool Regime
   C. No Partner in Crime for Asefi
   D. Enayet Convinces Asefi to Join Him

4. The main purpose of page 11 is to:
   A. show how often the religious police came to the gallery
   B. explain that watercolors can be painted on top of oils
   C. describe the factory building where the men rescued the art
   D. provide details about how they saved the paintings

5. The word 'them' in paragraph 1 on page 12 refers to:
   A. the art-rescue team
   B. watercolors
   C. the paintings
   D. the inspectors

6. The word 'anxious' in paragraph 1 on page 16 is closest in meaning to:
   A. disturbed
   B. withdrawn
   C. subordinated
   D. passionate

7. What does Sadaqui claim on page 16?
   A. His feelings towards the Taliban grew aggressive.
   B. He jumped in the fire to save the films.
   C. He risked his life to show his anger to the government.
   D. He was punished for his temper.

8. Who had the idea to save the film negatives?
   A. Sadaqui
   B. Kirimi
   C. Mustafa
   D. the entire group of filmmakers

9. A large wallboard helped _____ Afghanistan's film archives safe.
   A. stay
   B. maintain
   C. keep
   D. confirm

10. Which of the following is closest in meaning to 'persistent' on page 22?
   A. coherent
   B. determined
   C. abstract
   D. rigid

11. According to the writer, the public's sorrow when the Taliban regime collapsed was because:
   A. They believed that cultural treasures had been lost.
   B. The reign of terror and destruction was over.
   C. They were worried about the integrity of the new government.
   D. It was impossible to flee the country.

12. Why did the artists keep their black-and-white identification cards?
   A. to remind them that the Taliban might come back
   B. to remember how much they risked for their art
   C. to keep a historical reminder of the Taliban regime
   D. because they plan to make a film about their experiences

When Art Becomes a Victim

D uring the years when the Taliban regime ruled Afghanistan, thousands of people were killed and much property was destroyed. However, the Afghan people also suffered another kind of very important loss—the loss of irreplaceable works of art. Some, like the giant statues of Buddha at Bamiyan, were simply destroyed by the religious police. Many others, however, were sold to collectors and shipped out of the country. Obviously, the loss of cultural heritage for the country is tragic; however in addition to Afghanistan, situations like this exist in many war-torn countries, including Iraq. They have also existed in the past, including in Europe, during and after World War II.

McGuire Gibson and Henry Wright inspect returned items at the National Museum in Baghdad.

No one knows for certain how many of Iraq's precious historical and artistic treasures are now lost because of the recent war. During the early days of the conflict, attention was focused on objects being taken from the country's major museums, some of which have been returned. However, as time passed, researchers began to realize that perhaps an even greater loss was occurring elsewhere in the country. People were digging up important historical and artistic treasures that had been buried for thousands of years. Because of the chaos in the nation at the time, the robbers were able to remove these valuable items and ship them out of the country. Many of these national treasures may never be found or returned to their rightful home in Iraq.

During the period of Nazi domination in Germany, many works of art, such as paintings, statues, books, coins, and other valuable objects, were taken by the government from well-established public galleries as well as private collectors in Germany and elsewhere. Some items were placed in museums, but many others were put in secret storage, where they have yet to be discovered. Many items were also taken from museums in

"No one knows for certain how many of Iraq's precious historical and artistic treasures are now lost because of the recent war."

the Soviet Union and the Netherlands. Immediately after World War II ended, a second type of artwork theft began to take place. Before they left the country, occupying armies began their own form of stealing. Most of the theft involved individuals taking works of art for their own personal collections. However, some of the artwork taken by the Nazis and discovered by the occupying armies actually ended up in the control of foreign governments. Talks are still taking place between Germany, the U.S., Russia, and other countries over the true ownership of these works of art.

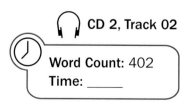

CD 2, Track 02

Word Count: 402
Time: _____

Vocabulary List

acclaim (3, 27)
accomplice (8, 11)
archive (2, 3, 15, 18, 19, 21, 22, 24, 27)
brutal (8, 12)
Buddha (3, 4)
carving (2, 4)
conceal (18, 21)
contempt (8)
deception (3, 12, 15, 22)
disable (21)
ditch (16, 22)
film negative (18, 19, 21, 22, 24, 25)
fundamentalist (4)
grab (16)
heritage (2, 4, 24, 27)
hit home (7)
ingenuity (3, 8, 15, 27)
landmark (2, 4)
oil painting (2, 3, 7, 11, 12)
plague (8)
plot (3, 11, 12, 21)
pound (16)
slash (7)
watercolor (3, 11, 12, 13)

Metric Conversion Chart

Area
1 hectare = 2.471 acres

Length
1 centimeter = .394 inches
1 meter = 1.094 yards
1 kilometer = .621 miles

Temperature
0° Celsius = 32° Fahrenheit

Volume
1 liter = 1.057 quarts

Weight
1 gram = .035 ounces
1 kilogram = 2.2 pounds